Creating

Confident

Communicators

By Trish Springsteen

Creating Confident Communicators

By Trish Springsteen
Copyright 2010 Trish Springsteen

3rd edition 2018 by Trish Springsteen

Published by MJL Publications

17 Spencer Avenue
Deception Bay QLD
Australia 4508
deb@mjlpublications.com.au

Disclaimer:

Produced by Trischel Holdings Pty Ltd 2014

ISBN: 978-0-6484221-1-2

⊠ Points to Ponder

If the best real estate is all about 'location, location, location'; then the mantra for running the best business has got to be 'communication, communication, communication'. – Sir Richard Branson

trischel
innovative communication training

Trish Springsteen
Public Speaking Coach, Mentor and Author

Table of Contents

Introduction

The Importance of Good Communication Skills

COMMUNICATE – Impart, transmit (feelings, news, a discovery) Oxford *English Dictionary*
COMMUNICATION – The act of imparting or transmitting.

Communication is fundamental to all working relationships, but bad communication causes more controversy in business and industry than any other factor.

As organisations grow bigger communication deteriorates. The larger the organisation the more impersonal communication can feel. With some government departments and multi-nationals employing millions of people lines of communication become stretched and can break down.

At the same time people expect to be treated as individuals, they need to be consulted, informed, given the opportunity to air their points of view and to have those opinions respected. Attempting to bridge this gap is the role of the good communicator.

In business, these issues become even more important, because at the core of every business, regardless of the industry, are people; and people need to communicate. A company's success depends on communication. Employees face an endless exchange of ideas, messages, and information as they deal with one another and with customers day after day. How well they communicate can determine whether a company quickly grows into an industry leader or joins thousands of other businesses mired in mediocrity.

The Cost of Poor Communication

Information provided by Project Management Institute, in the US[1] shows that ineffective communication cost companies time and money, and equally important it impacts on their reputation. In fact, recent research shows that "only one in four organizations can be described as highly-effective communicators". The PMI report quantifies this – "ineffective communication puts US$75million at risk." Can organisations really afford ineffective communication? What are they doing about it?

The effects of miscommunication are further highlighted by information from Gallup, McKinsey and AonHewitt in the US[2]. Gallup notes that "Disengaged employees cost the U.S. more than $500 billion each year in lost productivity". McKinsey report that "Organizations can improve productivity by up to 25% by connecting with employees". AonHewitt notes that "For every 1%increas in employee engagement, you can expect to see an additional 0.6% growth in sales for an organization".

We still have the problem that many Managers, worrying about poor sales, customer dissatisfaction and increasing costs, still feel that communication problems within their organisation are far less important. They fail to recognise that in most cases it is the **ineffective communication** that is the basic cause of all these other problems.

And yet, a typical manager would spend up to 80% of their time engaged in some form of business communication, whether that is oral or written. Communication provides the critical links between the various functions of any organisation.

In fact so important is communication to business that Robert Kent, the former dean of HarvardBusinessSchool has said *"In business, communication is everything!"*

The latest Towers Watson Study for 2013-2014[3] confirms that "Companies that are highly effective at both communication and change management are three and half times more likely to financially outperform their peers than companies that are not highly effective at either".

Organizations that communicate
more effectively have more
successful projects.

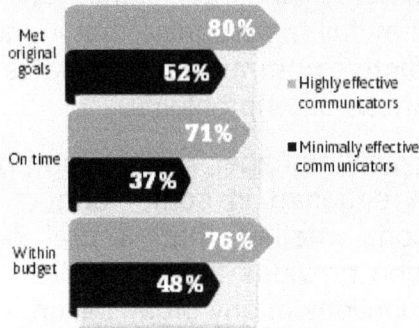

Met
original
goals
80%
52%
■ Highly effective
communicators

On time
71%
37%
■ Minimally effective
communicators

Within
budget
76%
48%

Source: ©2013 Project Management Institute, Inc. *Pulse of the
Profession In-Depth Report: The High Cost of Low Performance: The
Essential Role of Communications*, May 2013. PMI.org/Pulse

Today it is important to note the trends in public
relations and marketing. How you promote your
organisation or business to your clients will impact
on how you connect with them. Of interest is the
trending use of digital storytelling and social
listening. Verbal communication ranks in the top five
important skills to cultivate for the future. (2017
Global Communications Report – USC Centre for
Public Relations)

Video is an important component of communication
today. Interact in "8IC trends for 2017: what's
happening to internal communications?" reports:
"93% of internal communication professionals
believe video has become essential".

Introduction

What does this mean for organisations and businesses?

Whilst the increase of and improvement in electronic communication technology means communication is becoming easier and more efficient, the importance of effective communication and speaking skills is becoming even more apparent. Technology merely provides us with the equipment – it is still people who have to formulate the communication; and they can really misunderstand how to achieve effective, coherent, confident communication.

⬧ Points to Ponder

"To bridge the communication gap, organizations must help everyone learn to say the right things to the right people in the right channels. " – *PMI White Paper Communication: The Message is Clear* December 2013
http://www.pmi.org/~/media/PDF/Knowledge%20Center/Communications_whitepaper_v2.ashx

"90% of all management problems are caused by miscommunication." – Dale Carnegie

Chapter 1

Creating a Communication Balance

Trischel's Two Principles of Communication

Principle No 1 - Conversation is not Communication

"The single biggest problem in **communication** *is the illusion that it has taken place."*
George Bernard Shaw

So why do we get it so wrong – why do we have this illusion that we have communicated when all we have done is confuse?

One reason we get it so wrong in business is because we confuse conversation with communication. There are whole rafts of cultural rules that govern the way we speak with each other. There are taboo topics, there are certain ways of addressing people that are considered downright rude, and often we use euphuisms to disguise our message and to lessen its distressing impact. *"Our cat passed away last night,"* Instead of saying *"The cat died".*

Sometimes we will tell a downright lie, especially if the truth will get us into trouble! *"How do I look in this new dress"* is an exercise in terror. If I tell the truth I am going to be in it up my neck, and if I lie I am going to feel guilty for the rest of the day. What to do? Most of us choose the easy way out – "*You look fine, dear!*"We make these choices because conversation is used to build relationships.

Now we can't do that in business. If we indulge in the social niceties of conversation we can be in trouble. We can't decide to withhold information in case it may upset someone. We can't fail to disclose something because it may be embarrassing to us. We can't disguise the truth and we can't tell a downright lie; the cultural rules that govern conversation are out of place in business.

To be effective, business communication needs to be clear, concise and most important of all it must be correct! We can't dress it up in nice little boxes and pretend that it's something else. And yet, that is what so many people actually try to do. They take the conversational skills that they have learned through family, school and friends and try to create a communication style that answers businesses' needs. Unfortunately it doesn't work. Used within the business environment conversational communication can create chaos – at best it leads to misunderstanding and mistakes.

If you are trying to maintain the credibility and professionalism of your organisation then you absolutely must apply some critical appraisal of your communication standards. If you are, or you recognise that your staff are trying to communicate important instructions, essential information and critical data in the incorrect way you could be one of those businesses who are losing out.

Principle No 2 – Balance is Everything

To be effective all communication needs to be balanced between the intellectual input and the emotional connection.

Unlike conversation, which is designed to build and enhance relationships, business communication is designed to:

- Inform
- Instruct
- Inspire

... and sometimes we use all three purposes in one communication!

Most business communication has a specific purpose; it has a distinct outcome that is required. Sales presentations are an excellent example. When a sales rep gets up to give a presentation on a new product they have one clear aim – to sell the product.

Now to do that they will need to **inform** the prospective client about the new product; they may also have to **instruct** on the performance, and they will certainly need to **inspire** them to purchase.

To achieve the desired outcome, our sales rep will need to appeal to their intellect with the information, and to create an emotional connection to clinch the sale.

Too often we get this balance wrong; and I am sure that we are all familiar with the speaker who has all the facts and figures at his finger tips; and who drones on and on boring us to tears. We have all the Intellectual information that we could need – but really, who cares? What's in it for me?

Then there is that passionate life-style guru, whose presentation excites and energises us to the point that we want to get and out and start creating the new 'me' right now! But we can't quite remember how to do it. We have been overwhelmed by the high intensity emotional connection – but we're a little light on facts.

What we need is a balance between the two aspects to create really effective communication. What we really need is some kind of memory jogger, to remind us that both sides of the communication needs to be addressed – what we need is the Trischel formula for **balanced communication**

$$EC = Ic + Ec$$

Where effective communication (EC) is achieved from applying the Intellectual Content (Ic) **plus** the Emotional Connection (Ec) - and only then will we be able to create an effective communication process using all our skill that will inform, instruct and inspire - that will, in fact achieve our specific aim. Note: there does not have to be equal components of emotional connection and intellectual content but there does have to be some component of each. Sometimes there will be more intellectual content – facts and figures, other times more emotional connection – what is in it for me.

⊠ Point to Ponder

"Know the difference between Conversation and Business Communication. To be an Effective Communicator you need Intellectual Content and Emotional Connection." – Trish Springsteen

Chapter 2

Creating the Communication Process

The really sad truth about communications is that what you believe you have said is not the point. What is important is what people think you have said and how the message has been received.

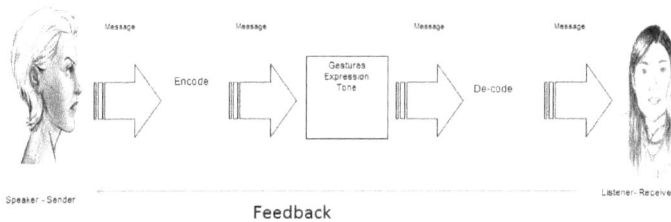

For communication to be successful, the listener needs to understand the message exactly how the speaker intended. It is not necessary for the listener to agree with the message as long as they understand it.

Miscommunication – or Communication Breakdown

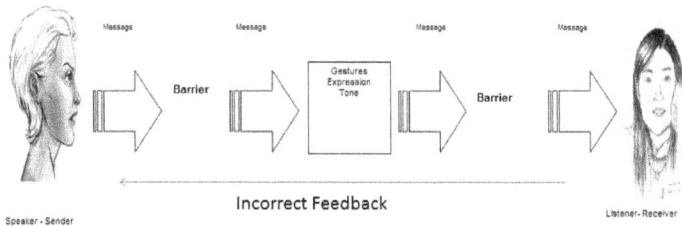

Breakdown in Communication is costly to business. It wastes time, money, credibility and importantly customer goodwill. The effect of miscommunication on the team can be reduction in morale, a breakdown in teamwork and personality conflicts.

Communication Breakdown is usually caused because the listener did not receive the message as the speaker intended due to incorrect de-coding. There are many reasons for this, often misinterpretation is the key to misunderstanding, and throughout this book we will be looking at ways in which you can overcome this by ensuring that your tone of voice, your body language and your gesture enhance and support the message without distorting it.

Effective communication is vital to the quick and accurate transmission of information and instruction. Effective communication is one of the most important elements in avoiding mistakes which costs business time, money, productivity and vitally credibility. For me, it's loss of credibility which can have the most impact: easy to lose and very hard to rebuild.

While much communication in business today is conducted by electronic means, it is the personal communication skill – the public speaking – which in the final analysis is the most effective way of communicating your information, your message or your instructions.

This is why I am going to focus on your personal communication skills - The skill that allows you to express your point of view, to impart your knowledge clearly and concisely. .

So Effective Communication is a simple practical skill that can be learnt. Public Speaking is the tip of the communication iceberg. Confidence and skill in public speaking translates to effective communication and confidence that your communication will achieve your goals and outcomes.

In this book I will help you to improve your ability to sell your message by organising your information; I will show you how to persuade people of your point of view by promoting and defending your ideas; and how to enthuse and motivate groups to adopt your proposals.

All these skills form the art of communication, but it is the two easily learnt principles developed by Trischel, which will improve your ability to communicate, not just at work, but also in the social sphere.

▣ Points to Ponder

"Developing excellent communication skills is absolutely essential to effective leadership. The leader must be able to share knowledge and ideas to transmit a sense of urgency and enthusiasm to others. If a leader can't get a message across clearly and motivate others to act on it, then having a message doesn't even matter." — Gilbert Amelio, President and CEO of National Semiconductor Corp.

"Leaders who make it a practice to draw out the thoughts and ideas of their subordinates and who are receptive even to bad news will be properly informed. Communicate downward to subordinates with at least the same care and attention as you communicate upward to superiors." — L. B. Belker

Chapter 3

Creating Confidence by Controlling Nerves

"According to most studies, people's number one fear is public speaking. Number two is death. Death is number two. Does that sound right? This means to the average person, if you go to a funeral, you're better off in the casket than doing the eulogy." ~ **Jerry Seinfeld** (American actor and comedian)

Understanding Nerves - Nerves are energy which manifests itself in the familiar symptoms of dry mouth, shaking hands, sweaty palms and all the rest of the debilitating feelings which makes it difficult for us to perform to our best ability.

We need to understand that the symptoms of performance anxiety and the symptoms of exciting anticipation are exactly the same; the only difference is in our attitude to the activity which causes them. They are two sides of the same coin – which side will you be?

The key to controlling nerves is in understanding that everybody, regardless of their expertise or experience, suffer from nerves. Some of the greatest actors in the world suffer the same fear and dread as we do. Sir Lawrence Olivier was so badly affected that he kept a bucket in the wings – to handle the nausea! But it did not stop him performing. Lord Olivier said that his 'nerves' was the thing that added the fire and spice to his performance. And if we can learn the tricks of the trade, as he did, we can use our nervous energy to add fire and spice to <u>our</u> performance.

Before the Presentation

1. Thoroughly prepare and rehearse your presentation. Familiarity with the subject will give you confidence.

2. Familiarity with where you are speaking and who you are speaking to will also help with the confidence. If possible, visit the venue prior to the day. Check out the speaking area, check how you will approach it, where is the audio visual point? Plan where your lap top will go and how you will present your visual aids. Will you need a microphone? If so, what type is it, and if possible try it out. This pre-presentation check will take away the sense of the unknown and is a good practice where it is practical.

If it is not practical, then make sure that you arrive at the venue well before your presentation time and make all the checks then. Give yourself every chance to succeed. Don't forget to make sure there will be a jug of room temperature water with a clean glass provided for you and check where it will be placed. Extremes of temperatures can affect the vocal chords.

Ask a few questions to find out more about your audience – how many will be there, what is the message you want them to take away, is there anything particular that the organisers want you to include?

3. Use visualisation to have a test run. Visualisation is one of the major mental preparation tools for champion athletes as well as performance artists. Mentally visualise what will happen on the day. This is where checking out the venue well prior to the presentation adds dynamics to this process. Picture yourself sitting, waiting to be introduced. Imagine your sense of anticipation. Your notes are all in order, you know that your equipment is working perfectly (you have checked of course). You are fully prepared-and then the introduction. Visualise yourself walking confidently towards the speaking area. You are so excited to be giving this presentation that there is a smile on your face. The applause is generous and welcoming. You shake hands and place your notes on the lectern. Comfortably in position your raise you head and smile at the audience. You see yourself giving the presentation – you are awesome, then you finish and hear the applause. Well done.

If you believe that you will be confident and successful – it is more likely that you will be.

4. Use distraction therapy. When you find yourself dwelling on how scared you feel, try to think of something that gives you pleasure. Re-run that great day sailing; remember that fantastic sunset in Bali. Choose what you want to think about and dismiss other thoughts from the mind. This prevents the 'fear factor' – the building up of tension and anxiety to an overwhelming level.

5. Rehearse your physical exercises. These, if performed on the day, will keep your nervousness in check.

a.   Practice tensing your muscles until they start to quiver, then let go. You willfeel an immediate sense of release.

b.   Drop the head, let the cheek muscles go loose, open your mouth and waggle your jaw. This will dissipate any tension around the jaw line.

c.   Yawn a few times, with your mouth as wide open as you can get it. This not only loosens the jaw, it activates the mucous membranes and prevents that dry mouth.

d.   Take a few deep breaths. Inhale slowly to the count of four; hold the breath for a four count; exhale as far as you can then rest. Do this once or twice, but if you start to feel a little dizzy stop.

Use these preparation tricks <u>before</u> you even get to the venue. Then when you do arrive you will have a sense of total control.

During the Presentation - Tricks to Continue in Control

So you've prepared your presentation carefully, and you have done the exercises in part one. You are on the stage and – oh no – your mouth goes a little dry. There is a slight shaking of the legs and your first words come out quivery. What on earth can you do with this misplaced nervous energy?

1. Deliberately look at the audience. Yes, those scary people out the front. A good deliberate look will show you that they are smiling at you, willing   you   to   succeed.

2. Dry mouth? Remember the jug of water you arranged to be on hand? Help yourself to a glass of water and take a drink.

3. Extremities Beginning to Shake? Take heart; just transfer the nervous energy creating the shakes into positive body movement. Change your foot position. Raise your arms to make a deliberate movement of greeting. If it strikes during the presentation deliberately change your position on the stage. If your hands start to shake, drop your arms to your side and clench

your fist tightly – then let go. There will be that immediately sense of release you practiced well before.

4. Oh dear – Quivery voice? Take a controlled breath; hold it and begin speaking on the exhale at a slightly lower pitch. Using exhaled breath will help to lower your pitch; and if you can concentrate on speaking just that little bit slower you will soon have that voice back under control.

5. Heart Pounding? – No, the audience cannot see it, and while your heart is pounding you know that you are alive and well!

6. Dry Ticklish Throat – if this is a possibility for you, make sure that you have the water ready.

7. Sweat rolling off the forehead and dropping on the notes? – Simply pause, and say "Excuse Me" and wipe it away from your face with a big cotton handkerchief that you have previously tucked into a pocket, or placed near the lectern.

8. Make sure that you really wipe – just taking little dabs won't work, and you will be forced to get the handkerchief out again and again. So make it one big wipe that should solve the problem for some time. And please, do not use a tissue.They stick to sweaty foreheads and leave a trail of tissue shreds sticking to the damp

spots. This does nothing to enhance your credibility status with the audience.

9. The dreaded nausea – it might be worth your while to visit your doctor for a prescription for an anti-nausea drug if this is a real practical problem for you. Mild nausea can be controlled by breathing, re-focussing the thoughts and sips of water.

10. Making mistakes or fumbling words – All professional speakers, radio announcers and TV anchors have fumbled their words, got the words in the wrong order fairly regularly – so why should we be perfect? At an Australian Labour Party meeting one of our previous Prime Ministers was introduced (so the story goes) as Ruddy Kevin!

If it is just a minor fumble, don't bring attention to it by apologising, just continue. If you got the word, name or whatever totally wrong, pause repeat the correct word with a smile. The smile shows the audience that you are aware of the problem and puts the audience on side.

If you find that you are fumbling a number of words, it is probably because you are speaking too fast. Take a deep breath, tense up and let go and relax. Continue the presentation, focussing on the message, and slow your speaking down.

Following these suggestions and tips should help you change that nervous apprehension into excited anticipation. If all else fails – pause, smile and they will smile back.

⟨X⟩ Points to Ponder

"Grab 60 seconds of insane courage. Believe in yourself. Don't be selfish – remember it is not about you –it is about those who need to hear your message, your communication, your service." – Trish Springsteen

Chapter 4

Creating Concise Impromptu Responses

"It usually takes more than three weeks to prepare a good impromptu speech." ~ **Mark Twain**

Unfortunately we don't have three weeks to prepare our impromptu responses. They will drop on us out of the blue. Usually at meetings, someone will turn to you and say "And what do you think of the idea?" Alas, the concise reply which would have seen you achieve greatness will not occur to you until at least two hours after the meeting finishes – usually while driving home!

So how can we manage to respond quickly and competently to an abruptly posed question that we don't have three weeks to prepare for?

Before Meetings

This is where those awkward questions can be anticipated. Ask yourself "What is on the agenda? Is there anything that applies to my position or my department? Are there any controversial issues which I may be asked to comment on?"

Make notes about your answers and decide what you want to say about topics you think may be referred to you. What information do you think may be required? What facts or figures could be important? Make sure that you have them in your briefcase or easily located on the lap top.

You are going to be meeting a client – prepare, have the information you need with you. Think about what you are going to say and brainstorm any potential questions.

So you have made some preparations, but how can you structure the response so you sound in control, competent and make it clear and concise?

<u>Before getting to the Point</u>

Before we really start to work at our response we need to make sure that we really understand the question. So:

1. Listen to the question carefully. Many people actually only listen to the first five to ten seconds of the question before they start working on the response. This can mean that we answer the question we thought we heard rather than the question which was asked. So listen all the way through before anything else. What if we are not sure precisely what the question actually is? Then we clarify. We can do this by asking the question back "*If I understand you correctly what you are*

asking is ....." or*"I am not sure if I understand exactly what it is you want me to comment on"* or even *"Could you repeat the question?"*

2. Next, ask yourself the simple question *"What do I know/think/feel about that?"* If the topic is completely unknown to you just admit it. *"I am sorry that is not something I am familiar with."* If it is something that we need to obtain further information on, then say so. *"I am sorry I am not sure about the figures on that, I will check and get back to you"*

But if you do know the answer, hold a point of view or have a decided opinion, then the answer to your question should be the main point of your response. And once we know what it is we are going to focus on, it is time to start constructing our reply.

Introducing THE FORMULA

The Formula is a simple and easy-to-remember way of structuring an impromptu response which will allow you to stay focussed on the topic. We call it "The PREP Factor" – which is short for *"Prepare to Dazzle them!"*

P The **Point** of your response– it's the answer to the question you just asked yourself. This is the personal point of view or the vital piece of information sought. It is the WHAT you think, you believe or you know; and shows that you understand what you are talking about – You are ***informative.***

R The **Reason** for your Point -this is where the reasons for your point of view or opinion are explained. This is the facts, the figures, the reasons and the logic part of your response. Sometimes our response needs explaining, terms need defining, the importance of the subject can be clarified, and background information could be briefly touched on to make our Purpose clear.   All this helps to show that you are a ***credible*** source of information.

E The **Examples/Explanation**of points – Personal examples of your meaning, or to highlight your points of view are the best way to demonstrate your response, " *Let me give you an example of what I mean*" will show why your opinion is correct, or why the information is vitally important, or why the procedures needed changing. When you can cite personal experiences and stories to explain and demonstrate your point of view, you become a ***believable*** source.

P Restate your **Point**– this is a brief recap of your main points, or your opinion, which rounds the response off and gives your listeners a clear indication that you have finished your reply. You have responded ***concisely.***

This simple formula is the basis for most information communication. We can use it to construct our presentations, write our report, make our email concise and understandable or in any other situation where clear communication is required.

It explains in straightforward terms what we know, think or feel, and why that is so. We make our information credible with facts, rational logic, before being relevant with explanations of how it affects us or fits into the bigger picture before making it personal with anecdotes or quotations. Finally, restating the purpose of speaking again signals to our listeners that we have completed our response

This time, when driving home instead of going over what you should have said, you can bask in the achievement of what you did say.

⊠ Point to Ponder

"If you know that you are going to a meeting, make sure that you consider all possible questions or opportunities to speak – and prepare for them." – Trish Springsteen

Chapter 5

Creating Competent Concise Speech Introductions

This is possibly the most common speaking assignment that can be passed to us. *"Oh, by the way would you please introduce the new Marketing Manager; he would like to say a few words."* Simple isn't it?

Actually while a good introduction can make it easy for the following speaker, a bad introduction can leave the audience confused and, more importantly, reluctant to listen.

So what is the best way to address this situation? We need some kind of routine which will ensure that we cover everything that a good introduction needs. These are:

Why This Speaker?

The audience needs to know who is giving the presentation. In addition they will want to know why they should listen to him or her. What experience do they have and what qualification do they possess that makes them a credible speaker on this topic?

Why This Subject?

Again, the person making the introduction needs to make it quite clear to the audience why this subject is important, and exactly what the topic is about.

The Relevance to The Audience

A speaker giving a 20 minutes presentation at a seminar is taking 20 minutes of their audience's time. There must be a reason for speaking, and that reason should be relevant to the audience. It may not be immediately apparent to the audience, which is why a good introduction clearly points it out to the audience.

So those are the three major issues that should be covered by any introduction. But there are one or two tips for success which will help you put together a professional introduction to make the speaker's task much easier.

What to do when Introducing a Speaker

1. Get the name right! This can be really difficult if the name is pronounced differently to the way it is spelled. It this is the case make sure that you write the name down phonetically – this will alert you to the difficulty and allow you to pronounce the speaker's name accurately.

2. Try to use the speaker's name once or twice within the introduction so that the audience will understand it.

3. Speak clearly and do not rush. The speaker has spent time and trouble on their presentation and deserves an equally well prepared introduction.

4. Make sure that your introduction ends with the presentation's title – and then the speaker's name. This ensures that the last thing the audience hears from you is the name. Then lead the applause. A wise presenter will inform the speaker that he will close the introduction this way so the speaker is ready to move on cue.

5. Turn to the speaker and smile; wait until he reaches the speaking area and shake hands before returning to your seat.

6. It is possible that the speaker may refer to your introduction at the start of the speech so be alert and show your appreciation of his remarks with a smile and a nod in response.

And then there's what not to do!

1. Don't try to outshine the speaker.

2. Don't tell the audience the main focus of the speaker's presentation, or try to summarise the whole of the speech.

3. Don't rely on memory – you are sure to get the name   wrong   if   you   do.

4. Don't ad lib. Spontaneous comments can be disastrous – especially after a few drinks. In fact don't drink prior to a speaking assignment. The disaster potential outweighs the lack of fear factor.

5. Don't highlight any problems the speaker may have. *"We are delighted that Steve has almost recovered from his heart attack and is able to be with us tonight".* Most audiences will now sit through the presentation waiting for Steve to collapse.

6. Don't build up the speaker to unachievable heights. *"Joe is one of the best in the business, he is probably the greatest speaker I have ever heard – and the funniest too!"* This type of introduction puts huge pressure on Joe, which he will not thank you for.

7. Avoid introduction clichés like the plague! – Lose these:-

a.... who needs no introduction

b. Without further ado

c. We are honoured to have ….. with us today

d.… our speaker's 'better half' or even worse ' his
      good wife' - it begs
the question, where is his bad wife?

e. **Heeeere's** ……………. and finally

f.. None other than …………

⊠ Point to Ponder

*"Tartle: act of hesitating while introducing someone
because you've forgotten their name."* – Common
Scottish term

Prepare your introductions!!!

Chapter 6

Creating Clear Presentations and Speeches

When a man's knowledge is not in order, the more of it he has the greater will be his confusion. ~ Herbert Spencer

And ours! Planning is a major part of successful presentations. However before we start to plan out ours, we need to work out what it is we are talking about and what it is we need to achieve. Luckily, within the work place we are often assigned a subject for our delivery; but even so there should be some solid foundation work done before we get to the planning stage.

First – Before we even sit down to work on our presentation we need to be absolutely clear what we need to achieve. And even if we are given a topic, we need to fully understand the purpose of the presentation.

For instance, we may have been asked to give a presentation on *The Importance of Public Transport*. That sounds straight forward. But what is the purpose? Is it merely to inform people of what is available locally; or are we trying to convince people to leave their cars at home and use it; or perhaps we want to motivate our listeners to support our attempts to improve it.

Each one of these relates to the *Importance of Public Transport* – but each one has a different purpose. It is the **purpose** of the presentation that will determine the type of information you use; and the **purpose** of the presentation will set the goal to be achieved.

In our example of *The Importance of Public Transport* the first purpose will have been achieved if the listeners are much better informed about the services available in their location. In the second one, we will have succeeded only if a larger number of people use public transport than did so before. Sometimes these results are nebulous. Finally, we will know that we have achieved our aim if our audience flocks to sign our petition.

In each one of these examples the outcomes were entirely different; but the topic was the same. If you are asked to deliver a presentation make sure that you are absolutely clear on what is required to achieve – your goal, your outcome, the message you want the audience to take away. Only then can you decide what information will be required to achieve it.

Researching a subject can be fascinating, and we can spend hours on the internet, at the library and talking to experts. But whatever information we choose to use it must be pertinent to achieving the aim. If it is not we must discard it.

So using as an example our topic *The Importance of Public Transport,* perhaps we are concerned about the problems of pollution. Our concern could be that there are far too many cars on the roads today and that we can improve the situation by using public transport as our first choice. So our General topic is *"The Importance of Public Transport"* and our special perspective could be *"Reducing Air Pollution"*

With this in mind, we can now go to our research tools and find out how many cars are presently on our roads; what is the current level of air pollution; what are the pollutants that car engines discharge into the air. You might research cities where cars are banned from city centres and see how the figures have changed.

You are looking for supporting information for your point of view. It could be that all this information modifies your original approach, if so, write down any changes to the general topic or to your specific perspective.

What about pertinent quotations – these are always good to support your view point. Eventually you should have enough information to understand the present situation and to support your special perspective. It is now time to start planning the presentation.

We should have a structure that looks like this:

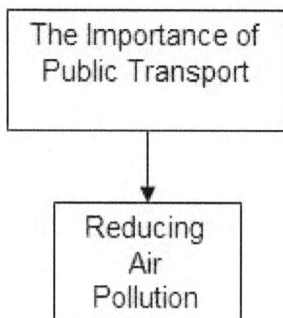

```
┌─────────────────────┐
│   The Importance of │
│   Public Transport  │
└─────────────────────┘
           │
           ▼
    ┌──────────────┐
    │   Reducing   │
    │     Air      │
    │   Pollution  │
    └──────────────┘
```

We need now to consider just how much time we have been allowed to deliver this presentation – after our research we will probably have far too much information and will need to prune it severely. No matter how difficult it may be, we should always keep the ultimate aim of the presentation in mind. I often print out the aim of my speeches, what it is I want to achieve - and attach it to my computer so that it will bring me back on track on those occasions I am tempted to stray.

OK we now have heaps of information, and all of it relevant to the aim of my speech or presentation - So just what are we going to say?

Time is always going to be limited, and the attention span of our audience is likewise limited. About ten minutes is about all an audience can take without a change of pace, or some interaction or some distraction. Within that time frame you will only have time to present three main ideas or main points. If you try to make more than this your audience will be unable to retain the gist of your arguments. You will have overloaded them and **you will lose their interest**. Information overload is one of the main causes of ineffective communication.

For speeches of longer duration - say for 30 minutes - it is better to prepare three ten minute presentations; each self supporting but all moving towards the same outcome. While we still have the basic structure, what we also have is more time to develop our arguments. We also have the luxury of being able to recap before moving on.

So we will work on the basic building block - the ten minute presentation; and the next part of our planning is to decide the three main telling points, which will support your argument and convince the audience.

Using our example, perhaps the first main point could be a summarised outline of the present situation. We could look at existing numbers of cars, highlight the pollution levels and consider the problems this is causing. This could be *The Present Problem.* We could then discuss what may happen if we do not take steps to address the situation – we could call this *The Future Problem* and finally we might suggest that there is something we can do about it right now. – *The Present Solution.* This would lead directly to the aim of the presentation – get out of your cars and onto the bus!

Putting it in our plan – we can title our main points to complete the basic outline.

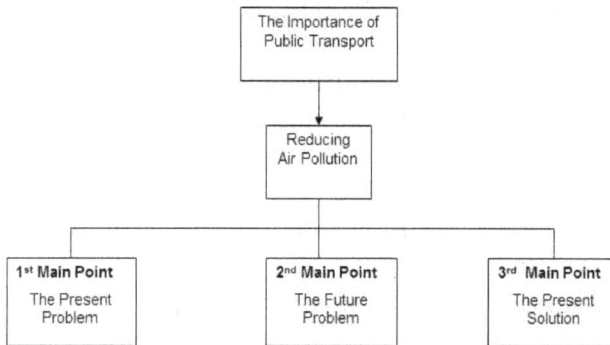

```
          ┌─────────────────┐
          │ The Importance of│
          │ Public Transport │
          └─────────────────┘
                   │
                   ▼
          ┌─────────────────┐
          │ Reducing         │
          │ Air Pollution    │
          └─────────────────┘
                   │
     ┌─────────────┼─────────────┐
┌──────────┐  ┌──────────┐  ┌──────────┐
│1st Main  │  │2nd Main  │  │3rd Main  │
│Point     │  │Point     │  │Point     │
│The Present│  │The Future│  │The Present│
│Problem   │  │Problem   │  │Solution  │
└──────────┘  └──────────┘  └──────────┘
```

This basic structure should allow us to present our material in a logical sequence which our audience can readily follow. Now we need to go back and select our information to support our three main points. And remember we have a time constraint. The most difficult part of arranging our research material is an unwillingness to throw any of our cherished quotations or information out – but we should always be asking the questions "Does this enhance my point of view?" "Is it vital to my position?" "Does it really support the theme or the idea I am presenting?" "Will it achieve my goal/aim?" If the answer is "NO" then discard it.

It is time now to consider what we will include and there are a number of techniques you can use when presenting your main points or arguments.

First, *FACTUAL*, that is supplying facts and figures to support your point of view. The difficulty with this is that people often do not retain figures unless they are written down. Anyone who has had to sit through a sales conference, or listen to a Treasurer's Report will appreciate that most of it will float away into the mists! Also, figures that are outside of a normal person's experience will have very little impact. Instead of saying that it was 300 metres long, you could try *"three semi-trailers could be parked end to end and still leave room"*. Again, expressing your information as a percentage can often make it easier for an audience to comprehend. *"82% of Australians have no knowledge of their own constitution"* however, be careful of using percentages which may not support your statement. *"35% of today's society supports increased police powers"* is not a convincing argument in a speech arguing in favour of this. Someone is bound to point out that in fact 65% do not!!

Second, *ANECDOTAL*, or describing a case of human experience. If your speech concerns the plight of the homeless, realistic information about the true conditions faced on the streets would be crucial, particularly if your anecdotal information comes from a clearly recognised expert. For instance, *"The*

Salvation Army tells us that one family...". Where your information is obtained from other sources, it may be supportive of your argument to name them ... *"As Thomas Paine said in his book "The Age of Reason..."* or *"The Report on 'The Condition of the Environment', issued by the State Government in 2008 clearly shows that..."* Audiences are more impressed by your statistics if you assign sources to your information – it avoids the *"Says who?"* reaction.

Finally, *PERSONAL STORIES.* Where your own personal experience can be used to illustrate and support your argument, the audience has an immediate sympathetic response. You are there, you have done this, seen that, experienced something and you are telling us about it. It is an immediate personal response that cannot be surpassed by any other technique. Stories are powerful, memorable connections to the audience.

So now our structure is taking on a more solid form:

```
                    ┌─────────────────┐
                    │ The Importance of│
                    │ Public Transport │
                    └────────┬────────┘
                             │
                             ▼
                    ┌─────────────────┐
                    │    Reducing     │
                    │      Air        │
                    │    Pollution    │
                    └─────────────────┘
```

The Present Problem	The Future Problem	The Future Problem
Examples Facts & figures Anecdote/Quote	Anecdote/Quote Researched statistics Examples	Anecdote/Quote Researched statistics Examples

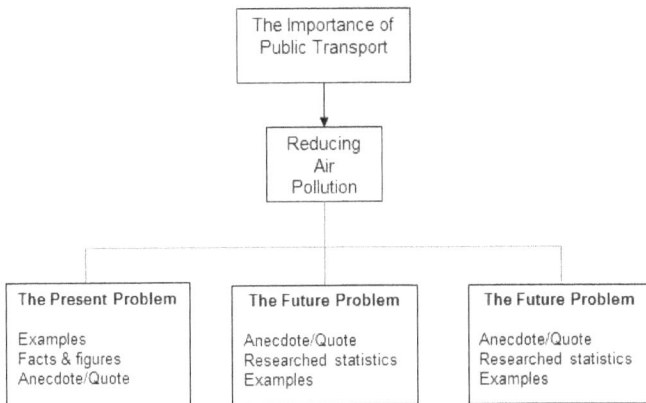

This takes care of the subject and the logical sequences – and you should have a clear direction to achieve the desired outcome; but it is really only the beginning.

A Speech consists of three basic parts, first *The Opening,* which should grab the audience's interest and introduce what it is you are about to say; secondly, *The Body,* which contains what it is you are saying; and finally, *The Conclusion,* in which you summarise what it is you have said and leave the audience with a clear idea of what you want them to do with your message – a Call to Action.

Let's have a look at them in detail:

THE OPENING

Always open with the actual introduction to your topic. You have already been introduced so there is no need to reintroduce yourself. Do not apologise for *anything,* most audiences don't notice what is so glaringly obvious to you. By apologising for leaving something out, for instance, you immediately draw their attention to the fact you have forgotten something.

Quotations For a speech about self-awareness the quotation *"To be or Not to be"* could be woven in as an effective opening statement. Or if your topic is responsibilities versus rights, perhaps JFK's quote about *"Ask not what your country can do for you .."* may be an appropriate opening. You might have discovered a really pertinent quote during your research – if so open with it. When you restate it later the audience will have a sense of recognition.

Questions Always a thought-provoking opening. A question immediately involves the audience, as the general response to being asked a direct question is to consider your answer. For instance, *"What would you do if someone you loved asked you to help them to die?"* as an introduction to a speech concerning euthanasia would make the audience consider their own position carefully. However, when using this opening technique it is important to allow the audience TIME to consider their answer, so after posing the question, **PAUSE!**

<u>Dramatic Statements</u> If these are short and sharp, they can be very effective attention 'grabbers". Such dogmatic statements as *"I hate Rhubarb"* or *"In my opinion those who mistreat animals should be reincarnated as a dog!"* are statements that are flexible enough to be able to be worked into almost any topic -   but remember, they must lead somewhere, and they should be a way of introducing your main theme or topic.

Next comes the **Body** of the speech, which we have already in detail – it's our planning document – so finally we reach …

THE CONCLUSION

The closing part of your speech is where you are able to reinforce your arguments, and tie all the points together in one strong and powerful conclusion which is focused on achieving the aim. This should be the time when you encourage your audience to **consider** something..."*doesn't this make you think that in a country as rich in resources as we are...*" to **change their opinion**, "*perhaps what I have said will make you think again about just lying around in the sun this summer*"; or to **do something**, "*so let us all make a resolution to recycle all our household waste from now on!*"

In our example of *The Importance of Public Transport* the conclusion to the first purpose may be to hand out new timetables; the second, a call to arms to *Get out of the car and onto the Bus*; and the final one – *Come and sign this petition demanding improved services.*

In the conclusion you repeat the **purpose** of your speech, and if you have used one of the opening hints we have suggested, an excellent way to round out your topic is to return to the opening gambit. "*Let us consider how JKF's remarks can be useful in today's society*". "*Perhaps your answer to my opening question would be different now*" You could also finish with a return to your speech title; in a speech entitled *Justice or Law*" your conclusion could be a reiteration of your three main points, and then perhaps *"considering the difficulties in understanding some of the recent legal decisions, perhaps it is natural that to believe that Justice and Law have very little in common!"*And be prepared for 'discussion'!

The conclusion of your speech **IS NOT** the place to introduce any new material into your presentation! It **IS** the place to recap and call for action.

Now you have the information you have researched well organised to support and convince your audience of the logic of your ideas. What to do now? Rehearse, Rehearse, Rehearse. Check the timings – it is important that you do not run over your allotted time. You may have to cut material from the body until you meet your time. A good idea is to plan you speech to conclude a few minutes early – this allows for interaction from your audience. When you do a speech live it nearly always goes longer than when you practised. You are now fully prepared to deliver an informative and interesting speech to riotous applause!

⊠ Points to Ponder

*"My advice to you concerning **applause** is this: enjoy it but never quite believe it!"* –
Samuel Lover

Chapter 7

Creating Confirming Body Language

When the eyes say one thing, and the tongue another, a practiced man relies on the language of the first. - Ralph Waldo Emerson

Using confirming body language and gestures will create an air of confidence about you. And this is not something that you can read about and do it – it needs as much practice as your speech does. Practicing the speech from the concept of stage presence should give you a clear understanding of the impact of the speech on your audience.

You need to realise that your audience does not start making assessments of you when you start talking. They will watch the way you approach the speaking area, are you confidently striding, or nervously shuffling? Do you look happy to be here – is there a big smile on your face? If you approach the lectern with a smile your audience will be inclined to smile back at you. This has a twofold advantage; first it will make you feel more confident as a smiling audience creates far less tension, and secondly, an audience that is smiling is warming towards you and that makes convincing them much easier. They are far more willing to agree with someone they like.

How you stand when you face an audience projects its own message. It is your posture that reflects your attitude and whether or not you are confident. In addition, a good posture helps you to breathe properly and to project your voice effectively. A good relaxed stance also provides you with a good starting point from which to move in any direction. It is your base.

The same air of confidence should be used when entering the Board Room for a meeting, walking into a team briefing, going into a client meeting or attending a network meeting. Project confidence and belief in yourself, your expertise and your message and that is the impression your audience, client, other attendees, board members will receive.

Having reached the speaking area what to do now?

First, re-position the lectern if this is necessary, you may have to ask someone to adjust the heights – remember if you have checked out the venue first you will know all this needs to be done and it can be organised prior to you approaching the lectern.

If you are using notes place your notes on the lectern and make sure that they are in order and easy to see. Never staple notes - having to remove notes from the lectern to fold over pages will distract your audience. Merely place the notes on the lectern with page one on the left hand side, and the rest of the pages on the right hand side. To change pages just slide the new page across and over the previous page. This can be done without the audience noticing anything. Note: It is perfectly okay to use notes – all speakers experienced and not have used notes at one time - it is **HOW** you use the notes that will determine if you are presenting a confident persona.

If you are using a microphone, this too should have been checked prior to now. To check the sound level, do not tap the microphone or blow into it – it causes damage. Just repeat the usually phrase – "For a sound check, testing – one, two, three"

Now take up the speaking position. Stand up straight but not too relaxed, with your feet about shoulder width apart. Try putting one foot slightly ahead of the other, and balance your weight evenly on the balls of your feet. If you are particularly nervous and your legs are shaking, place the rear knee up against the back of the other knee. This will lock the knees together eliminating shaking and swaying.

Lean forward very slightly, relax your shoulders, but be careful not to let them droop. Keep your chest out and your stomach in. Your head should be erect and your chin should be slightly raised, but make sure that you are comfortable. Let your arms hang naturally at your sides, with the fingers slightly curled.

Now take a few deep, full breaths. Make sure that you feel comfortable. Your posture should be alert without being stiff. If this position doesn't feel natural for you try repositioning your feet slightly until your body feels balanced.

You are ready to present and connect with your audience

Gestures

A gesture is a specific body movement that reinforces your spoken message. A gesture can also convey an abstract concept or a particular emotion. There are a number of ways you can incorporate gestures or body language into your presentation, but usually they are made using the hands and the arms. During conversation we will use our hands to add expressive emphasis to our speech; and hands can be wonderful aids to communication, in fact in our natural conversations most of us will use gestures naturally and spontaneously. Shorn of self-consciousness our gestures are an outcome of the subject and our interest in it.

However, as soon as we stand in front of an audience, the agonising feeling of self-consciousness steals over us, and like many inexperienced speakers we are unsure of what to do with our hands and arms. Putting them in pockets or behind backs does nothing to solve the problem. And unfortunately, when beginning to add gestures to the presentation some people can over gesture, waving their arms around like someone being attacked by a swarm of wasps! The secret is practice, practice and still more practice until your gestures feel smooth and natural.

We have the ability to use an infinite variety of individual gestures, however many Australians of Anglo-Saxon cultural descent find it difficult to be open and expressive; while other cultures, such as those of the Middle East or Southern Europe, use their hands freely and expressively when they speak. The specific gestures we make as well as the meaning we assign to them is a product of our cultural training, and some innocent western gesture, such as the making of a circle with the thumb and the forefinger to indicate approval, is considered to be obscene in many areas of the world. It is therefore important that the gestures you use mean the same thing to your audience as they do to you.

Why Gesture?

- Gestures add a visual component to our presentations. They reinforce your message and can help the audience to understand the unspoken emphasis of your message.

- By painting a visual picture for the audience, gestures can add a dramatic component which focuses and clarifies the audience's understanding.

- Gestures can also help your audience to understand the major points of your message, and be a sort of visual punctuation.

- By using gestures in the opening parts of your speech you can use the physical activity to dissipate nervous tension.

- By adding a measure of visual interest you can help maintain your audiences focus on the speech and you as the speaker.

Types of Gestures

While there are infinite varieties of gestures, all can be grouped into four main types

1. Descriptive gestures – which are used to clarify or enhance a verbal message. They can help the audience to understand contrasts, comparisons, visualise size, shape, movement, location and number.

2. Emphatic gestures – used to underscore the message. They indicate earnestness and conviction; for example using a clenched fist suggests strong feelings such as anger or

determination. Especially useful in passionate speeches and presentations.

3. <u>Symbolic gestures</u> – used to demonstrate or create a mood. An open palm suggests giving or receiving, while a shrug of the shoulders indicates unconcern or ignorance.

4. <u>Prompting gestures</u> – these are used to evoke a specific response from the audience. If you wish your audience to raise their hands, or clap or perform some definite action then enhance the chance of a response by performing the action yourself first.

Gestures made above the shoulder level are said to be '**strong gestures**' and tend to suggest physical height, inspiration, or emotional exultation. Gestures made below shoulder, referred to as '**soft gestures**' are used to indicate lowness, rejection, apathy or condemnation. Those made at or near shoulder level suggest calmness, serenity or anything that is balanced, whether it is mentally, emotionally or physically.

How gestures can be interpreted can be shown by considering the simple gesture of holding out your hands towards the audience. Done with the palm held upwards often means the act of giving or receiving – the exact meaning depends on the verbal message being delivered. If you repeat the action with the palm held downwards the sense of secrecy, completion or stability can be conveyed. Holding the palm outward towards the audience immediately indicates halting, repulsion, negation or abhorrence. By holding the hands perpendicular to the body with palms facing each other you can indicate a measurement, contrast or compare things. So with one simple gesture many messages can be sent.

How to gesture effectively

Gestures should be an outcome of your own personality and the message that you are delivering, however, the following six rules can be an effective way to start on your use of gestures within your presentations.

1. Respond Naturally to What you Think, Feel and Say – In normal conversation it is natural for you to emphasis your words with gestures to some degree or other, a speech is a larger

conversation, so try to include those gesture which come naturally while you practice. If you are naturally an energetic speakerwith a tendency to wave your arms around don't try to inhibit it, but if this doesn't come naturally to you try rehearsing in front of a mirror and watch for those natural movements which instinctively arise out of what you are saying, and then build on them.

2. <u>Create the Message for the Gesture, not the Gesture for the Message</u> – a good gesture comes as a response to the spoken word, when you are delivering a speech, if you are passionate about the subject then the gesture should come as a natural outcome of the message. Involvement in your subject lessens any inhibitions and allows your natural tendency to take over.

3. <u>Suit the Action to the Word and the Occasion</u> – If you allow your natural gestures to emerge because of your involvement with your message then you would not have the problem of a gesture being contrary to the verbal message. People instinctively recognise when the message and the body language is in opposition and will inevitably believe the body language. They may not understand why it is that they do not believe you, but they will know that somehow you are untrustworthy.

In the same vein remember that strong emphatic gestures should go with strong emphatic statements, and softer more fluid gestures should accompany lighter, softer statements. Don't use a sledgehammer to crack a nut!

Note also that the larger the audience or auditorium the larger and more expansive your gestures need to be.Create them with more emphasis and at a slower rate. And also the position in which you are required to deliver your speech may affect the type of gestures you are able to use. As a guest after-dinner speaker, the top table position may restrict the use of wider expansive gestures – these could put at risk the speaker's fellow diners!

4. Make your Gestures Convincing – When you use gestures they should be animated, lively and appropriate to the message. If you start having doubts about your gesture half way through it you will send an unconvincing message to your audience. How to be positive about it? Every gesture is a total movement from the shoulder and never, ever from the elbows! Elbow gestures can make us appear like penguins! Move the entire arm away from the body in a free and smooth movement. Wrists and fingers should be relaxed and supple. Nervousness will make them tense and stiff, but this can be overcome

by **practice**. Effective gestures are broad enough to be visible to all.

5. <u>Make Your Gestures Smooth and Well-Timed</u> – There are three parts to a single gesture, *the approach, the stroke, the return.* During the approach the whole body begins to move in anticipation of the gesture. The stroke is the gesture itself, and the return is simply bringing your body back to balance.

    The flow of the gesture through from balance, approach, gesture, return, balance should be executed like a dance movement, each part distinctive, but a part of the whole. And just as good timing is essential in comedy, so too in a speech the stroke should be performed on the precise word to make it effective. However, there are various ways in which the approach can be varied to intensify the gesture. Begin the approach well in advance of the gesture, holding it until the exact instance of the stroke and returning to balance by simply dropping the arm to the side.

6. <u>Make Natural, Spontaneous Gesturing a Habit</u> – .   Firstly eliminate distracting 'instinctive' movements from your speeches.

Some of the really distracting habits are such things as:

- Rattling keys or loose change in the pockets

- Twisting a ring

- Fiddling with your watch

- Constantly pushing your glasses up the bridge of your nose

- Playing with a pen or pencil, especially clicking a biro

- Twiddling a piece of hair

If you find yourself doing any of these make a conscience decision to STOP. Then find those natural movements that enhance your presentation, and start to build on them. Develop them until they become naturally wide, expansive and positive. Adapt them so that they can be used to emphasise strength and softness. Watch other speakers to see what works for them, and see if you can incorporate that movement into your natural way of gesturing. What works for others may not always be right for you, experiment and see what works. You will soon find that you will be using a completely new range of gestures and movement based on your natural manner, which can enhance and strengthen your speech and your message.

What is Body Language
Chapter 7
Creating Confirming Body Language

Moving across the stage, moving about the speaking area is the most highly visible physical action you can perform as a speaker. When it is used purposefully it can be very good and very effective, but when it is bad it is extremely distracting. So never move without a reason.

Whenever you use a body movement during the speech it brings the audience's immediate attention to you. So by making your movement mirror the message, you not only grab the audience's attention, you also enhance the impact of the message.

It is tedious to watch a stationary object, - hence the saying something is as interesting as 'watching paint dry!' but at the same time over enthusiastic use of body movement can be extremely distracting, and the audience is tied to watching what you are doing as opposed to listening to what you are saying. The aim is to strive for the middle ground – just enough to keep their attention yet not enough to drive them nuts!

If you are nervous it is a good idea to incorporate into your opening, a definite, strong body movement and gesture which is designed to enhance your opening remarks and which will negate any nervous tendency to indulge in the 'nervy fiddles'

<u>What types of body movement can you use?</u>
Stepping forward towards the audience during your

speech indicates that you have arrived at an important point that you want to share. Taking a step backwards tells the audience that you have completed that point, and you are giving them a chance to digest it before moving on. Walking across the speaking space can either mean you are moving from one point to another, or that your point is so important that everyone needs to hear it.

Using Facial Expressions

A poker player is the only one who should cultivate a deadpan expression; to a speaker it is a barrier between them and their audience.

People watch a speaker's face, particularly the eyes, while they're speaking, partly because of politeness, but mainly because this is the way in which they receive the precise information to make the message more understandable. Facial expression is often the key to determine the '*exact*' meaning being delivered.

For example, if a friend smiled broadly at you and said *"You're crazy."* Would you be offended? Probably not, but if the same statement came accompanied by a sneer, or a look of disgust, what then? The same message delivered with a different facial expression can cause a vastly different reaction in the listener.

Your facial expression will show the audience how you feel about your topic, and they will make an assessment of sincerity on whether they trust your body language. Also, your facial expression will extract a mirror response from your audience, smile at them and they will smile back. Scowl at them, and watch out; nod your head to emphasis a point, and you will notice members of the audience doing the same. Remember, what people do will affect how people feel, and how people feel affects what they believe.

Unfortunately nervous tension can be unconsciously released by moving facial muscles, licking the lips, biting the lips, twitching the mouth or gritting the teeth are all examples of some of the distractions which can occur.

Another unconscious facial movement, which is often a problem for inexperienced speakers, is the 'unconscious frown'. While this is probably due to nerves, to the audience it often is interpreted as unfriendliness or arrogance. An unconscious frown can occur when you have tried to memorise the speech word for word, and are having trouble remembering the next one!

<u>What is the easiest solution for all these problems?</u> It is simply to **SMILE**. A smile releases facial muscle tension, a smile induces a similar response in the audience, and a smile can relax your nerves as well. Once you have your audience on side, you can launch into the prepared speech with gusto.

Eye Contact

Using eye contact is the best way to involve your audience in your speech. By using good eye contact you make your speech and its message a personal experience for the audience. No matter how large the audience is, each member takes it personally when they feel that you are speaking directly to *them.* If you fail to make eye contact with some members of your audience they will feel ignored and excluded and will probably resist the logic of your message

Most people tend to believe people who look them straight in the eye; if you don't, it can be interpreted as insincerity or even dishonesty. So how can you establish good eye contact with all your audience?

1. <u>Know your Material</u> – If you have to continually check your notes, or return to the lectern to find your place, any bond you have established with your audience will be destroyed. If you know

your material well and can work without notes and away from the lectern you can build up a bond of empathy with your audience which will add to the impact of your message. If you have to use notes, make sure that you constantly re-establish contact with your audience.

2. <u>Establish a Personal Bond with your Listeners</u>. - You do this by speaking to a particular person. In a large auditorium if you choose one person to address your remarks to, all the other people in the vicinity of that person will feel included in the rapport, so direct your remarks to one person  within a small group range and let the optical illusion do the rest.

Speak to each person for about five to ten seconds, or complete one sentence before moving on to the next person. Add gestures indicating the general position of the member of the audience, and all those in the immediate area can be made to feel that your remarks were addressed to them personally.

3. Monitor Visual Feed Back – Your audience will also be sending non-verbal messages of their own, and being alert to these responses you can gauge the audience's response to your presentation, and you can modify it accordingly.

If the audience is not looking at you, they probably aren't listening either. You will have to regain their attention possibly by the use of humour or by strong body movement. If the audience looks puzzled or perplexed perhaps they haven't understood the statements or arguments and you may have to provide additional explanation. Watch them as you explain and if they begin to register comprehension then move on to your next point. Is the audience frowning at you? Remember they can often mirror your facial expression, try smiling at them, and if they respond consciously try to lighten your facial expression. If they are fidgeting check if you are engaging in any distracting mannerisms, if not you may need to re-engage their interest with humour or a dramatic change of pace or emphasis. Strong body movement will usually refocus the audience's attention on the speaker.

When you have researched your topic, organised your material, rehearsed and practiced your speech until it becomes part of you, you have the foundation of a good speech. How to make a good speech a great speech? One of the greatest tools we have for exuding sincerity, confidence and emotion is the human body. With strong and confident gestures main points can be emphasised, emotion conveyed and sincerity demonstrated. Good body movement can maintain the audience's interest and help convey the strength of our conviction, and appropriate facial expressions will convince our listeners of the depth of our feeling for the topic. Include good eye contact to encourage every member of the audience to feel that this message is just for him, then you are well on your way to becoming an interesting, dynamic and convincing speaker.

Body language that is congruent with the verbal message is just as important in the Board Room, meeting with clients, attending a network meeting or creating your videos.

⊠ Points to Ponder

"Gestures betray a lot about the speaker's personality, passion and enthusiasm and can make or break a presentation." – Jamie Carter, *Everyone's a Public Speaker ... Even You!* 2003, Vocal Communications, Sydney

"There are four ways, and only four ways, in which we have contact with the world. We are evaluated and classified by these four contacts: what we do, how we look, what we say, and how we say it." – Dale Carnegie

Chapter 8

Creating Cadence with Vocal Techniques

We often refuse to accept an idea merely because the tone of voice in which it has been expressed is unsympathetic to us." ~ **Friedrich Nietzsche**

Our voice is a unique instrument with which we can play many tunes. The English language is said to be one of the most musical of the world, and yet many of us do not utilise the gift we have been given to the best of our ability.

How is your voice created?

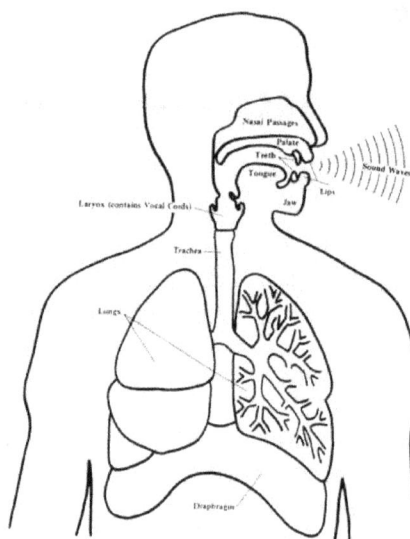

The most important thing to remember is that breath produces voice, and while this not a biology lesson, it is important that we have some idea of what creates the sounds we make.

Try this exercise: take a deep breath and hold it. Breathing in expands the abdominal walls and flattens the diaphragm. – you should be able to feel the physical tension. Now breathe out. This relaxes the diaphragm and contracts the abdominal wall – you should be able to feel the difference. The air we breathe out provides the controlled production of sound. This air rises and pushes against the vocal **chords** (*See Diagram)* causing them to separate for a moment allowing the air to pass between them. It

Chapter 8
Creating Cadence with Vocal Techniques

is the rush of the air past them as well as the elasticity of the chords themselves which pulls the vocal chords back together producing vibration, which is the basis of sound.

The difference in people's voices is caused by their **resonance** which is affected by the throat, the nose and the mouth. This is why your voice changes when you are suffering from sinus or nasal problems and when you have a sore throat.

People's unique spoken sound is a combination of the size of their vocal chords, about which we can do nothing, and the resonance which can be deliberately altered by a knowledgeable speaker.

But what is a Good Speaking Voice?

One of your goals as a speaker should be to develop a good speaking voice which has the following qualities :

- It is **pleasant** – conveying a sense of warmth

- It is **natural** - reflecting your personality, and sincerity

- It is **dynamic** – indicating force and strength

- It is **expressive** – portraying emotion, and indicating shades of meaning,

- and it should be **audible** – thanks to good projection, volume and articulation.

Before deciding how your voice quality can be improved or changed it is important to make some kind of judgement about your present voice. We can do this by considering some simple questions.

What kind of a voice do you have?

How Loud?

The loudness of your voice or its volume needs to be appropriate to the size and location of your audience. A deliberate change in the volume adds emphasis and impact to your message. But remember there is a difference between speaking softly for effect and inaudibility. A whisper is air without sound, but a fading voice is sound without air. Air causes voice projection.

How Expressive?

When speaking in a normal conversation everyone adds life and colour to their words - but under the added stress of speaking to a group many people can lose that spontaneity and find their speech comes out flat and wooden. Being able to alter the Pitch, that is the highness of lowness of your voice, will add depth to your presentation.

How Enthusiastic?

The amount of enthusiasm which you project with your voice indicates your voice quality. Plenty of enthusiasm indicates positive voice quality and this can motivate your audience to be receptive of your message. However, negative voice quality can tend to alienate your audience. The major cause of negative voice quality is tension – emotional or physical, so being able to control your nerves is an aid to changing your voice quality.

Also, be aware that smoking can also affect the quality of your voice, so if you smoke it might be better to wait until **AFTER** the speech before you light up.

Words are the building blocks of our messages, and we need to make sure that our audience is quite aware of what we are saying, After we have considered volume, the next stumbling block to understanding our message is bad articulation.

What is articulation?

It is defined as being how you formulate the words when you speak. Good articulation will prevent the dreaded mumbles disease, the symptoms of which are swallowed words and indistinct delivery.

The formula for good articulation is **P+E=A** where the **P** stands for **Pronunciation**. This is the formation and the way you say the words - having the right sounds in the right places. If we fail to do this, we suffer from mispronunciation which can change the meaning of what we intended to say, and can affect the way in which our audience perceives us. If in doubt of the correct pronunciation of a word, check it before you use it - particularly in technical presentations.

So Pronunciation PLUS **E** for **Enunciation** - and what the heck is THAT?

Enunciation relates to the fullness and clarity of the speech sounds,

So Articulation requires Good Pronunciation and Good Enunciation.

These can be achieved by

- Accurately forming the sounds,
- Usingenough breath to form the sound, and
- Completely finishing the sound.

How to Create Vocal Variety

To change our vocal variety we should be aware of the following aspects of our speaking.

1. How fast do we speak? This is our **Rate of Delivery**, and this is closely associated with your culture, lifestyle and personality, and can often be the most difficult to change.

   Speaking to an audience demands that you deliver your message at rate which is easy for your listeners to understand. If you speak too fast you can frustrate you audience because they never have time to digest your information, and will give up the task. A speaker with too slow a rate of delivery makes it difficult to maintain interest and concentration, and as people think much faster than they speak you will lose your listeners.

   The most effective rate of deliver falls within the range of 120 to 160 words per minute. This rate is easy to maintain without rushing and slow enough to allow your audience to fully understand what it is you are saying. By deliberately varying your rate within your presentation you can add emotion and emphasis to your words.

2. As I have said, the English Language is spoken in musical tones, and a good speaker can use up to 25 different notes to convey the precise meaning or to add variety to their speech. Monotonous speakers will often only use two or

three. **Pitching** your voice up or down can change your delivery dramatically.

3. **Volume** is created by air, and air is produced by using the correct breathing technique.

4. **Timing** depends on practice, and on being able to listen to how other good speakers deliver their speeches. The use of pauses is one of the most effective weapons in emotional speaking, pauses can add emphasis, allow time for laughter to subside, and allow the audience to think about a question you have posed. Also the **hesitation pause** can induce anticipation and expectation, a wonderful tool for dramatic presentations.

Inflection

One of the most important characteristics of speaking is known as **Inflection**. It is also referred to as 'stress' or 'emphasis'. Inflection means raising the pitch, or emphasis on a particular word to add stress to that word. It can be used to stress the word itself, or to change the meaning or implication of a sentence. Look at this simple sentence.

I DIDN'T SAY HE STOLE FIVE DOLLARS

Now just using those simple words, but adding voice inflection, try to answer the questions.

1. Was it you who said he stole five dollars?

The correct response would be '**I** (emphasised) didn't say he stole five dollars!'

2. Did you say he stole five dollars?

'I didn't say **HE** stole five dollars'

You can try these:

3. Why did you say he stole five dollars?"

4. Are you sure it was Five dollars that he stole?

Inflection is often the best way of indicating the exact meaning you wish to convey, and more misunderstandings are caused by the wrong use of inflection than by any other vocal trick.

So to improve your speaking voice, remember these three things:

Correct breathing- this will enable good volume and projection

Correct articulation – avoid misunderstanding because your audience didn't understand what you said. Pronunciation and Enunciation will ensure correct articulation.

Finally – Practice, practice, practice - How, READ ALOUD, READ EVERYTHING ALOUD. Read poetry, read newspaper articles, read anything and everything aloud. Only then will you begin to learn the "feel' of the English language, only then will you begin to recognise pitch, rate and timing, and gradually they will become an inherent part of your speaking voice.

And read stories aloud, especially children's fairy stories! Yes really! – Just think of all those characters waiting to be brought to life by the voice. What voice would you use to portray the 'Beautiful Princess'? What about the 'Handsome Prince'? – and who would not have fun with the 'Wicked Witch'?

Then, why not have fun with some tongue twister exercises – these are great to really work the muscles of the face, and the jaw. Try saying them with real exaggeration. This gets those lazy muscles (the ones causing mumblitis) working again and you will find that your articulation will improve rapidly.

Here are a few vocal exercises you can use to improve your speaking voice :

• **Breath control**

   Breath control is the most important exercise of all as shallow breathing produces weak and ineffective speaking.Try slow, deep-breathing exercises for periods of 5 minutes taking no more than 20 breaths in that time.

Inhale while slowly counting to three, filling your lower lungs. Feel your ribs expanding, slowly let your breath out and recite the alphabet in a slow and measured voice. See how far you get using one breath.

- **Resonance**

  Your resonance creates your personal vocal quality, and it can be improved by the simple act of humming. This will reduce hoarseness and clear your nasal passages. You will be able to feel the vibration in the upper nasal passages.

  Try this :

  The Rangoon Gang banged the Hong Kong gong until it rang with a thundering boom around Kowloon

  When you start to feel the vibration you know that you have good resonance, so now try saying the words **enemy, men** and **many** over and over until the vibration can be felt and listen to the change in sound.

- **Articulation**

  Articulation gives speech its degree of clarity and your words their precision.

  To improve your articulation, firstly work on your vowels, "A, E, I, O, U". Try to give them their maximum value.

  Practise and exaggerate the following words: **calm, rain, sigh, cool, owl, all & fur.**

  Elongate the vowel sound as in 'Caaaaaaaalm' or 'Coooooool'. This will help to define the sound and the shape of the mouth, lips and tongue while forming the words and retrain the face to create the correct sound.

  Consonants, the rest of the letters, tend to be beginnings, sustainers and finishers of words. These can best be practised by the use of those tongue twisters, which also provide useful practice in word separation. Try these:

  She stood on the balcony inexplicably mimicking him and welcoming him in.

  Take care with 'in-ex-plic-ably; and 'mim-ick-ing [rest] him' can also be awkward.

  This next one is a workout for the mouth and lips and needs absolutely precision not to confuse your 's's' with your 'sh's!' – so start very slowly and precisely, and only speed up when you've got your muscles warmed up.

As the sun shines on the shop signs, she seeks a shot-silk sash shop's summer sale.

Another tongue twister based around 'mmm' and 'whh' sounds. Almost, but not quite resonating. Take care again to form the sound precisely; so start slowly and build up gradually, get those lips moving on the 'Wh' sounds and hear the difference.

Meals on Wheels deals meek meatless meals in Whitsun's witless wheatless weeks.

- **Flexibility (Using the organs of speech)**

This is the workout for the facial muscles, lips and tongue.

The tongue can be exercised by rapid repetition of letters such as **r rrrrr** and **dddddd** (this will also involve the palate and teeth).

Lips can be exercised by repetition of ee, oo, ah or horse noises.

The lower jaw can be exercised by repeating **"My mouth is round like a cow chewing its cud."** To get the full value of this exercise,

exaggerate the movement considerably –
reducing to normal as you get more proficient.

The **palate** may be exercised by repeating
words like "**King Kong, King Kong**", "**Gong,
gong**", and "**Ng, Ng, Ng**". – the palate is a
resonator, which you will discover when you
give these sounds full value.

These exercises will assist in the correct vocal
development of words and sounds.

When speaking it is our voice that becomes the
channel through which our message is sent. We can
add much intensity, passion, pathos, excitement and
boredom simply by the way in which we use the
voice, and verbalise the message.

Learning to improve the quality of our voice adds
great impact to our speech; and after all that
research and planning, our thoughts deserve the
best medium we can provide for them.

⌧ Points to Ponder

*"Words mean more than what is set down on paper. It
takes the human voice to infuse them with the deeper
meaning."* – Maya Angelou

"The tongue can paint what the eyes can't see." –
Chinese Proverb

Chapter 9

Creating Compelling Motivation

It is hard for us to imagine the dark days of the Second World War, especially in Britain as they realised that now they had to face the might of Hitler alone. It would have been easy to give up, to convince themselves that they couldn't do it. But then there was Churchill! If ever there was a time for a motivational and inspirational speech this was it.

Here is the speech that, it is claimed, changed the war:

"I have, myself, full confidence that if all do their duty, if nothing is neglected, and if the best arrangements are made, as they are being made, we shall prove ourselves once again able to defend our Island home, to ride out the storm of war, and to outlive the menace of tyranny, if necessary for years, if necessary alone.

At any rate, that is what we are going to try to do. That is the resolve of His Majesty's Government-every man of them. That is the will of Parliament and the nation.

The British Empire and the French Republic, linked together in their cause and in their need, will defend to the death their native soil, aiding each other like good comrades to the utmost of their strength.

Even though large tracts of Europe and many old and famous States have fallen or may fall into the grip of the Gestapo and all the odious apparatus of Nazi rule, we shall not flag or fail.

We shall go on to the end, **we shall fight in** France,
we shall fight on the seas and oceans,
we shall fight with growing confidence and growing strength in the air,
we shall defend our Island, whatever the cost may be,
we shall fight on the beaches,
we shall fight on the landing grounds,
we shall fight in the fields and in the streets,
we shall fight in the hills;
we shall never surrender",

This passionate speech, which implored the British nation not to give up the fight, is regarded as one of the finest addresses in history. So what was it that gave Churchill the lion's roar?

Researchers concluded that his pauses and tone gave his voice a uniquely recognisable quality, while his allusions to down-to-earth metaphors struck a chord with listeners.

Simon Elmes, creative director of BBC radio said: "Churchill is deeply steeped in imagery, and imagination is a key: he talks about Adolf Hitler 'sprawling' across Europe, using images that were very powerful sound-pictures such as the gritty monosyllables of 'blood, toil, tears and sweat'."

Elmes added: "here was a man who loved music hall and was a showman. By using language every man and woman could understand, he could move and stir people.

So the aspects of this speech which we can use are really very simple:

- Be passionate about the subject – without this you cannot inspire others.

- Connect with the audience with simple and relevant metaphors – use imagery which the audience can identify with. Churchill used the image of 'duty' and the historical belief that Britain had never been defeated since 1066 to instil in his audience a conviction that the island could be defended 'again'.

- Use simple and direct language which is easily recognised "in the fields and in the streets".

- Use pauses – especially to create anticipation. If you have ever listened to a recording of this speech, you will notice the 'hesitation pause' after each "we will fight" – it is not long but just enough to set up a sense of anticipation for the next words.

- Emphasis and stress to punch the meaning home – "we shall **never** surrender".

- Create emotion by choice of words – "we shall fight to the death".

- Finally – note the effective use of repetition – it is the sonorous repetition of the words "We shall fight" which rolls like a drum through the speech that gives it the powerful sense of inevitability.

We are not all Churchill, but we can use some of the tricks that he used to make our inspirational or motivational speech equally stirring.

☒ Points to Ponder

Developing excellent communication skills is absolutely essential to effective leadership. The leader must be able to share knowledge and ideas to transmit a sense of urgency and enthusiasm to others. If a leader can't get a message across clearly and motivate others to act on it, then having a message doesn't even matter." — Gilbert Amelio, *President and CEO of National Semiconductor Corp.*

"You can speak well if your tongue can deliver the message of your heart." – John Ford

Chapter 10

Creating Change with Positive Performance Feedback (PPF)

Most organisations in today's business world have in place performance criteria. Detailed explanations can be obtained on what should be assessed, how to recognise underachievers and then counsel them for improvement. However, there are few writings in the managerial field that set down precisely how you can offer constructive feedback to employees to encourage improvement with a willingness to listen and to take on board the constructive suggestions.

All too often when staff members are interviewed for underachieving the manager or supervisor is focused on the faults, and so these become the first things raised in the interview.

If you consider how you would feel if as soon as you sat down you were told "*This hasn't been done, That is an unacceptable standard and you are always late!*" Our first defensive mechanism when facing attack is to get aggressive. This is not a good start to encourage improvement in performance.

It's Time for THE SANDWICH

This method allows you to raise issues with staff members without them becoming aggressive and rejecting your suggestions out of hand. What motivates people to improve? Usually it is a sense of recognition and appreciation. If we can harness that then we have a perfect way to offer Positive Performance Feedback.

1. Let's start at the beginning. It doesn't matter who you are, everyone does something effectively. By recognising that general fact and commenting on it at the start we tap into the person's sense of appreciation. By getting them on side we create a willingness to accept our request for improved performance.

2. Now, concentrate on the specific activity or performance that is under review. Again there must be some parts of the project which were performed satisfactorily so highlight those and explain why they worked well. Again, effort has been recognised and appreciated.

3. This is where those areas of performance which do need to be addressed and improved can be mentioned. By avoiding blame or accusations such as *:You didn't do … you failed to …. Etc"* we can approach the problem from the positive side. *"What you did was excellent **and** I am sure can be enhanced if you thought of adding……..,*

changing ……….. Updating ……..spend a little more time on …. Etc"

No one objects to suggestions for enhancing work performed, and will often add suggestions of their own to improve the project or performance.

4. Summarise the interview by mentioning the main points again, and then leave the staff member on a high with a final complimentary statement of what they are doing well. *"Thank you for taking the time to summarise just the main points of your report, I am sure that with your excellent research, it will be a valuable document for the planning committee."*

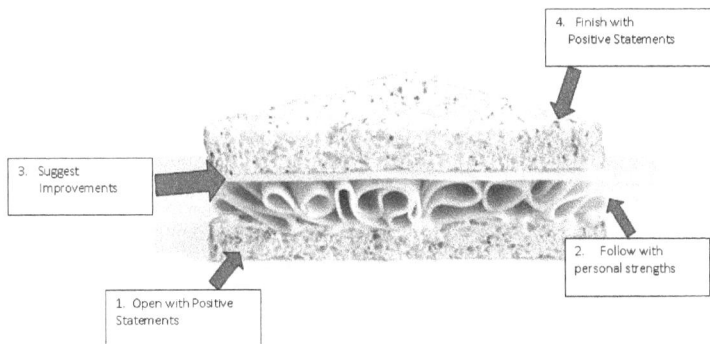

4. Finish with Positive Statements

3. Suggest Improvements

2. Follow with personal strengths

1. Open with Positive Statements

Giving **Positive Performance feedback** in this way means that we demonstrate our recognition and appreciation of work done, and instead of pointing out mistakes we offer suggestions for enhancement that can be used for improvement. Focussing on the positives instead of critical negatives allows the person to maintain dignity and self-respect and encourages improved performance – without resentment. That's got to be good for business.

⟨X⟩ Points to Ponder

"We all need people who will give us feedback. That's how we improve." – Bill Gates

"Take advantage of every opportunity to practice your communication skills so that when important occasions arise, you will have the gift, the style, the sharpness, the clarity, and the emotions to affect other people." – Jim Rohn

Chapter 11

Creating Clear Instructions

There's a common story in Outback Australia about a hapless tourist asking a local farmer for directions. After thinking a moment, the farmer rattles off a lengthy list of directions along the lines of "...take the old side road up past the Anderson's mailbox, and turn left when you see Smithy's cow. After a while you'll come to a broke-down truck, turn right and cut across the Williams' back paddock to the creek..." Inevitably, though, the farmer winds up concluding "but you can't get there from here!"

Much of our daily communication consists of giving instructions, whether helping friends find our new house or office or writing a manual for a new product or asking a work colleague to undertake a specific task. Since it is so common we should really be aware of the importance of good, clear instructions.

And yet, so many of the instructions we get are *so* bad. Electronics come with poorly translated manuals that are often more humorous than useful; software comes with thick manuals that sit, unopened, beside our computers for years; we finish assembling our flat-pack furniture with a handful of extra parts and doors that don't close right; and so on.

Giving good instructions, whether written or spoken, requires a certain kind of ability to be able to put ourselves in the place of a person who doesn't know how to do something — which can be difficult, especially when we can do it so easily and with little, if any, thought.

The Aussie farmer in the old story above gives great instructions — for himself. For the tourist, though, the instructions are meaningless — they depend too strongly on local knowledge that the outsider would have no way of knowing. He truly "can't get there from here", not without the local's specialized understanding.

Far too often when giving instructions, we start from an assumed knowledge base, as did the farmer above. We then build our set of instructions from this base and of course the person we are instructing falls at the first hurdle – he doesn't know the knowledge base we used so cannot use our instructions.

Or Projects need to be redefined, re-organised or re-done. If instructions were to be given clearly and correctly, and if the listener was able to query and confirm perhaps much of the 'down' time could be converted into 'up' time!

Another fact that often gets overlooked is that people take in information in differing ways. Some people find verbal instructions perfectly adequate; others like to have time to write down instructions or get a set of written instructions that they can read and refer to. And then there are those who are impatient of any instruction – they like to get in there and experiment.

Therefore, when considering giving instructions you may need to have back up. Have a set of instructions written out to support your verbal ones. Try to cover at least oral and written methods to improve your chances of having your instructions acted on correctly.

And use language that is easily understood. Instructions like "*the tochet bracket inhibitor must be placed in close conjunction with the empactic dessolier thusly!*" can have an odd effect on some people – it closes minds and eyes!

So what do you need to include in any set of instructions for them to be effective?

A good set of instructions must provide information about five things: let's consider it from **the listener's point of view**

- **Mission:** What do the instructions show me how to do? Am I fully confident I know exactly what is needed to be achieved?

- **Procedure:** What are the exact steps I need to follow to reach the destination and accomplish the mission? What tools and equipment will I need? What special information do I need to finish? Who will I have to help – if any? What backup is there for me?

- **Time:** How long will it take me to finish? – When is the project, etc required to be completed. (Other measures might be appropriate, like "how much money will I have to spend?" or "how far will I have to drive?")

- **Anticipation:** What difficulties should I expect to encounter on the way? How should I prepare for the project?; and

- **Failure:** What will happen if I screw up? What does failure look like?

Now let's look at some simple tips for giving good instructions:

- The procedure is probably the simplest part: break down the task into short steps and give them, in order, to your reader or listener. Remember, though, the lesson of the Aussie farmer: your listener or reader doesn't know what you know, or else they wouldn't need instructions.

- If you do not know the extent of the other person's knowledge, assume he or she knows nothing, and be sure to cover the most basic steps. If you do know the level of your audience's pre-existing knowledge, tailor your instructions to fit. In other words, break the task into the smallest, simplest tasks your audience will understand, and explain each step fully and literally.

- The time it takes to give instructions depends, obviously, on what you're telling or showing how to do. An important measure, though, is attention: how much time and energy can your listeners reasonably be expected to invest into a project. If it takes you half an hour to explain how to open a pack of biscuits, your audience will naturally get bored and stop paying attention.

- Remember that people retain knowledge in differing ways. If the task is practical, in addition to verbal and written instruction you might want to consider a practical demonstration, allowing the persons the time to try it out for themselves.

If there is more than one way to achieve the desired results, you could give the listener options.

- Always check to see if the listener has actually received the information **exactly** as you intended it to be received. *"Just to be sure I didn't leave anything out, let's reconfirm what I said."* Ask them to repeat back to you what the task is.

Ask questions like *"What should you do if ...... is not available?"*

- Give them time to ask questions themselves. Make sure that they are confident that they have the information they need to complete the task in the time frame allowed. If they have a problem ~ *"I doubt we'll be able to finish in the necessary time with Jim off on sick leave."* – address it. In this case, either extend the time allowed or roster another person to the team.

- The biggest difficulty in giving instructions is, as already noted, over-estimating what your audience already knows. Telling someone to remove a part on their car using a torque wrench doesn't help much if they don't know how to *use* a torque wrench, or even what one is.

- Problems can also arise when you fail to adequately describe a point — it often is not clear until several steps later that a failure has occurred, and the only thing to do for it is to trace your steps backwards until you find the error.

- And finally - **if the actual outcome differs from the desired outcome, your instructions have failed.**

Given how often we do it, you'd think that we'd all be able to give instructions pretty well. And we do, when we're giving instructions to our friends and family, for a good reason: we share quite a bit of our knowledge and understanding with them.

Where we fall down is when asked to give instructions to our employees or colleagues, to users of our products, to readers of our websites, and so on — people whose backgrounds, educations, and life experiences may differ sharply from our own.

If we are in business and in a position of some authority, it is inevitable that you are going to give instructions. It's part of the responsibility.

If we get our instructions right then we only have to do it once. But if we fail to get the proper information across to the person designated to actually do the task, then we will have to go back and start again.

The consequence of getting our instructions wrong can go further, the task may have been completed incorrectly or inadequately. If the former we may have a potentially dangerous situation and if the latter then it will have to be done again.

Either way, we have lost time and money, and possibly credibility.

So - Use the five types of information outlined above to make sure that you provide them with the information they need to buy or use your product or to complete the projects that both their success and yours rely on.

⟨X⟩ Point to Ponder

"Make sure you are all on the same level playing field before giving the instructions. Check for understanding and keep the instructions clear and simple." – Trish Springsteen

Chapter 12

Creating Connections Using Listening Techniques

While we might think that communication is all about the speaking, the hardest lesson we may have to learn is how to listen. Sometimes we just hear the first couple of seconds of what is being said and then jump in justify our point of view. This can be dangerous. If the person does not believe that you are taking their comments seriously you can lose goodwill very quickly.

Plus if you do not listen all the way through, you may misunderstand what the speaker says or means; which means you are responding to what you thought you heard rather than what was said – a dangerous practice.

On a personal note, one of the greatest relationship building tools is the art of good listening. Most people love talking about themselves, so if you are prepared to listen – you will have a friend for life. A good 'people person' is usually someone who listens.

Do You Know How to Listen?

Often we interchange the words "**Hearing**' and '**Listening**' as if they meant the same thing, but of course they don't.

- **HEARING** is thought to be passive – the act of receiving the sound through the ear, but we can often hear things without being really conscious of it. The early morning bird chorus can be heard, but is not often remarked upon. To differentiate between the bird songs we need to actively listen.

- **LISTENING** goes beyond hearing, Listening means that we try to make sense of what we have heard, we listen to get understanding. Active listening requires concentration on what is being said to distinguish the meaning. This is the ACTUAL message. To determine what this is we need to listen with our eyes as well as our ears. WHY?

When listening for understanding we need to focus on:

- Identifying main points and ideas ~ These are the main thrust of what the speaker is trying to say, and we need to clearly identify them

- Identifying the key words

The choice of words is vital to understanding the concept of the ideas; can we hear what these words are? Do we understand the way in which the speaker is using them? Do they mean the same thing to us?

Barriers to Effective Listening

In spite of our best intentions we may have already set up barriers to effective listening even before we walk into the room. Some of these are ~

- **TIME** – When time is short and getting shorter, we often don't want to be bothered with complicated conversation; or we can't be bothered with ideas or comments which we do not agree with.

- **PERSONAL MOOD** – Often the way we feel affects our ability to listen effectively. Worry, fear, anger and frustration will often cloud our attitude towards the speaker, or even the task of listening. In these cases, deliberate concentration is really needed.

- **ATTITUDINAL** – It has been said that the major barrier to listening is our natural tendency to judge, evaluate, approve or disapprove of the speaker. If we feel any animosity towards the speaker, or feel that they do not meet our personal standards (whatever they may be); we can allow our personal prejudices and bias to affect the way in which we receive their information.

As difficult as it is, once we recognise the problem we can chose to avoid personal prejudices by deliberately withholding judgement until the other has finished speaking.

- **LANGUAGE** – Difference in levels of language usage can cloud understanding. When a speaker obviously has English as their second language we really need to concentrate so that we can understand what the real meaning is – It may be necessary to clarify by asking a question back – *"If I understand it properly, what you are saying is ....*

Ways to Improve Your Listening Skills

1. **Show the Speaker that you are interested**. This means using body language to encourage the speaker. Looking interested is important, and as our faces show most of our emotion, we need to consciously be aware of how we are feeling. Giving the speaker positive feedback by nodding and looking interested will help to make the communication process two ways.

2. **Next, listen with your eyes.** We already know that a large part of the message is given with

non-verbal cues. Be alert to the speaker's body language and vocal intonation, these will warn us when something important is about to be said. A receptive listener will encourage the speaker to open up.

3. **Concentrate on what the speaker is saying**. Listen with an open mind, and analyse the information being heard. If necessary clarify what you think you heard by repeating it back in a different form.

Whether you are engaged in personal conversation or in business communication, improved listening skills will help you better understand the other's point of view.

All verbal interaction, conversation or communication, is a two–way process eventually. And after you have given your information; coherently, comprehensively and concisely – it is time for the interaction to begin. Feedback begins with listening to the other's point of view. It is not necessary for you to agree with it, but it is essential that you try and understand it.

☒ Points to Ponder

"Listening skills are an essential part of all communication." – Trish Springsteen

"Most of the successful people I've known are the ones who do more listening than talking." – Bernard M Baruch

Conclusion

Communication is important to businesses and to individuals. Ineffective communication can lead to loss of money, poor productivity, loss of time and what could be even more important the potential of loss of credibility.

A hidden cost of ineffective communication can be the loss of opportunities – either not stepping up to grab opportunities because of a lack of confidence or not making the most of opportunities because your communication could have been just that more effective.

The Communication Tips covered will assist in reducing the costs of ineffective communication and increase the effectiveness of making the most of opportunities that come your way.

So Remember:

- **Conversation is not Business Communication** – know the difference and know when to switch from conversation to effective business communication.

- **Balance is everything** - Effective Business Communication must have Intellectual Content plus Emotional Connection. It does not have to be in equal proportions – sometimes there may be more Intellectual Content – other times there may be more Emotional Connection but both elements must be there.

- **Effective Communication is a simple practical skill that can be learnt**. Public Speaking is the tip of the communication iceberg. Confidence and skill in public speaking translates to effective communication and confidence that your communication will achieve your goals and outcomes.

- **Create Confidence in Speaking** by becoming familiar with speaking, with your venue and know your audience. The more you get up and speak the more familiar you will become with the act of speaking. Visualisation and breathing techniques are valuable in overcoming your nerves. Practise, Practise, Practise. It's okay to be nervous – use the nervous energy to be a powerful communicator.

- **Concise Impromptu Responses** require listening, clarifying, thinking about what you know or your opinion and answering using the formula PREP.

- **Introductions to Speakers** require you to be clear and concise. Know the Speaker, the Subject and the Relevance to the Audience.

Conclusion
Creating Connections Using Listening Techniques

- **Creating Clear Presentations** require you to know your aim, your goal, what you want your audience to take away. The structure of your speech is important – an Opening that grabs your audience's attention and outlines your presentation, the Body that tells them what you want them to know and the Conclusion that sums up your presentation and leaves the audience with a clear call to action.

- **Body Language** provides the visual enhancement to your message. Gestures, eye contact, facial expression, stage presence all provide the emotional connection to your audience. People will more often believe the non-verbal over the verbal so ensure your body language is congruent to your message

- **Create Compelling Motivation** with simple and direct language, use of pause, appropriate emphasis and stress, powerful metaphors and words to create emotion. Be yourself and let your passion shine through.

- **Vocal Techniques** add the final dimension to being an effective communicator. Timing, pause, pitch, rate allow you to expand the emotional connection with your audience. If you cannot be heard clearly then your message cannot be communicated clearly. Take note of the speed of your voice, the articulation, how loud and how soft you speak. Do you have 'mumblitis'? Practise your vocal techniques to achieve your aim.

- **Positive Performance Feedback** communicated effectively to employees will encourage improvement with a willingness to listen and to take on board the constructive suggestions. Remember the SANDWICH method to ensure that the feedback is given in a manner that will produce the required response.

- **Instructions** form a vital component of your everyday communication. Giving clear instructions whether written or spoken, requires a certain kind of ability to be able to put ourselves in the place of a person who doesn't know how to do something. A good set of instructions should include details on Mission, Procedure, Time, Anticipation and Failure.

- **Creating Connections with Listening Skills** requires Active Listening. Know the difference between hearing and listening. Understand the barriers to effective listening - time, mood, attitude and language. Improve your listening skills by showing the speaker you are interested, listen with your eyes and concentrate on what the speaker is saying.

"Trish is an expert in the field of public speaking. I have engaged her services on two separate occasions and highly recommend her professionalism, knowledge and Trischel's training and mentoring services." **Juanita Anderson** Director Wasabi Marketing and Design

"Trish is an expert in her field and an informative guest speaker. She connects well with an audience and is generous with sharing tips and techniques. She trains in many areas however it was on the subject of 'How to Become Proficient at Public Speaking' that we invited Trish to address our recent Networking Luncheon in Hobart. I would have no hesitation in recommending Trish to anyone seeking to train and develop the skills of their staff." **Lynette Palmen AM** Founder and Women's Network Australia

"Trish - On behalf of my organization I would like to take this time to say thank you for your webinar/presentation on Effective Communication. I found the session very informative and look forward to implementing these tools to better assist my organization & colleagues in the future." **Shallene Amos** IT Training & Software Support Farmset Limited Papua New Guinea

References

1   PMI Pulse of the Profession In-Depth Report: The High Cost of Low Performance : The Essential Role of Communication, May 2013

2   https://dynamicsignal.com/2017/07/10/state-workplace-communications-companies-struggle-reach-employees-todays-disconnected-widely-distributed-workforce/

3   2013-2014 Change and Communication ROI Study Report Towers –Watson

Resources

Available for download from
http://www.trishspringsteen.com/contact/

Checklist: Preparing Your Presentation
Template: Organising and Presenting Your
Speech
Template: Introducing A Speaker
2-minute Training Videos

Join Trish's Community for ongoing resources,
ebooks, templates, information videos and
checklists

http://www.trishspringsteen.com/membership

Workshop Information available from:

http://www.trishspringsteen.com/workshops

If you have enjoyed this book, why not follow Trish's
thoughts on Communication, Leadership and
Personal Achievements on her blog at

http://www.trishspringsteen.com/blog

Trish can also be found on:

LinkedIn –
http://www.linkedin.com/in/trishspringsteen/
YouTube –
http://bit.ly/GetKnownBeSeenWebTV
http://bit.ly/TrishTalks
Instagram –
https://www.instagram.com/trishspringsteen/

About the Author

Trish Springsteen - Trish has had a passion for communication training since 1993. Having worked in both corporate and small business areas she had experienced firsthand the inconvenience and misunderstandings caused by poor communication skills by both managers and staff.

Joining Toastmasters was her own challenge to improve her personal skills and she soon found that she had a talent for training. It wasn't long before Trish was being asked to deliver motivational speeches, information sessions on improved communication to organisations and government departments. How she got into **Event Emceeing** is a mystery, but her vast knowledge of the Rules and Requirements for Business Meetings has become legendary.

She has a BBus (Health Administration); holds Cert IV in Training & Assessment and is an Accredited **Extended Disc** Practitioner. Trish is experienced in

leadership, **management** **communication,** **business skills** and is a highly sought after Personal Communication **Mentor**, **Coach** and **Speaker.**

Trish was the co-founder and owner of **Trischel,** a training company Creating Confident Communicators since 2006. It is now one of the most successful communication training organisations, training nationally and internationally. Trish has brought improved speaking and communication skills to introverts, authors, advocates, and bloggers. As well as communication, speaking and presentation skills to accountants from Crosbie Warren Sinclair; executives from The IQ Business Group and Aurecon; scientists from Rio Tinto Alcon; engineers from James Hardy and property retail experts from Jones Lang LaSalle.

Trish is Australia's Leading Expert in Empowering Introverts, a multi international award winner, host of Get Known Be Seen WebTV and international bestselling author of Step Up and Speak Out with Trish. Clients work with Trish because they know she can help them have the confidence and self-belief to make speaking easy, to step up Get Known Be Seen making it easy for their clients to find them.

Trish Believes in You Until You Believe in Yourself.

Trish is the author, co-author, contributing author of 14 books and is featured in **Motivational Speakers Australia.**

Book Trish to speak at one of your events and download Trish's Speaking Profile at:

http://www.trishspringsteen.com/book-trish-to-speak

trischel
innovative communication training

Trish Springsteen
Public Speaking Coach, Mentor and Author

www.ingramcontent.com/pod-product-compliance
Lightning Source LLC
Chambersburg PA
CBHW051737090426
42738CB00010B/2304